12 TIPS

FOR INTERNATIONAL STUDENTS LIVING AND STUDYING IN CANADA

By Monika Ferenczy
Horizon Educational Consulting/Conseillers en Education

FriesenPress

Suite 300 - 990 Fort St
Victoria, BC, V8V 3K2
Canada

www.friesenpress.com

Copyright © 2019 by Monika Ferenczy
First Edition — 2019

All rights reserved.

No part of this publication may be reproduced in any form, or by any means, electronic or mechanical, including photocopying, recording, or any information browsing, storage, or retrieval system, without permission in writing from FriesenPress.

ISBN
978-1-5255-4132-2 (Hardcover)
978-1-5255-4133-9 (Paperback)
978-1-5255-4134-6 (eBook)

1. EDUCATION, STUDENTS & STUDENT LIFE

Distributed to the trade by The Ingram Book Company

TABLE OF CONTENTS

v   Acknowledgments

1   Introduction

3   Family Structures and Siblings

7   Weather-The most important information to know while in Canada

15   Clothing

21   Customs and Cultural Transitioning

31   Food in Canada

33   Canadian Homes

45   Communication and Spoken Expressions

51   Transportation and Travel

57   Attitude and Motivation for a Successful Experience

59   Staying Healthy While in Canada

61   Personal Safety

65   About The Author

ACKNOWLEDGMENTS

Many thanks to the international students who inspired this guide including
Rodrigo Yan Chu, Gustavo de Paula Santos, Joao Victor Brandao, Ivan Melgares Mena,
Connor Liu, Zichen Wei, Yi Ma, Yan Wu, Kehan Li and Khoa Le,

those involved with assisting international students as hosts, teachers and agents
Claudette Andress, Jing Lui, Jennifer Olchowy, Alex Ma

and to many others for their valuable input and feedback.

INTRODUCTION

Canada is a large country of 36 million people from all over the world living within 200 km of the border with the United States. This diversity of people and culture helps make visitors feel they belong, and Canadians hope that you will feel welcome during your stay.

Canada is a young country having just celebrated its 150th birthday in 2017 and our flag, the Maple Leaf, is just over 50 years old. The symbols of Canada help residents remember the important events and meaning of being Canadian.

However, aboriginal people have been here long before Europeans came to settle here, beginning in the 1500s, mainly British and French settlers. Native Canadians are referred to as First Nations, Metis and Inuit (FNMI) populations and they are the fastest growing population in Canada, with the largest group of young people aged 15-25 and the fastest birth rate.

We hope you will enjoy the beautiful nature in whichever part of Canada you stay and that you have opportunities to explore your city and local neighbourhood regardless of the season in which you arrive.

FAMILY STRUCTURES AND SIBLINGS

If you are staying with a family, it may have:

One person – a man or woman is hosting you because he or she has room in his or her home and would like company and enjoys young people so that he or she is not alone.

A couple – they may have adult children who no longer live with them and enjoy having young people in their home for company and sharing Canadian culture with others. A couple may be two women, two men, or one man and one woman. Canada recognizes same sex marriages. Not all couples living together are legally married. If they live together for three years they become common law partners.

A young family where you may be the oldest and there may be a mother or father, or both, and one or more children who are looking to welcome a student in their home as a cultural experience and an older role model for their child or children.

Family with older children or teenagers the same age as you who want to get to know other students. Sometimes these families are not able to travel, so having students from different countries around the world helps them learn about different cultures.

Blended family where there are children of different ages from each adult from a previous relationship, who may come and stay on weekends regularly, but not stay every day with the family.

Extended family where there may be one or more generations of adults living in the home (grandparents or uncles and aunts or adult siblings) and children of various ages as well.

In Canada a brother or sister is a relationship between two siblings who have the same biological mother and father. If siblings have the same mother but not the same father, they are referred to as half-siblings (half-brother or half-sister). The same terms are used for siblings who have the same biological father but not the same biological mother.

HOMESTAY VERSUS PRIVATE BOARDING SCHOOL

There are two options to living and studying in Canada: one is a Homestay, which is when a student stays with a Canadian family in their home and attends public school. All international students under the age of 18 years must stay with a family and cannot live on their own. Many different Homestay organizations offer students this option with full room and board (a room and three meals a day) of half board (one meal and a room). Both options have a cost in addition to school tuition costs.

Private boarding school is a better option if a high school student is not comfortable living with a family. The school and living residence is in the same building or on the school property. For international students who have previously spent time learning in a boarding school setting, this option is an easier transition to studying in Canada. This option is only available for students completing high school. There are relatively few boarding schools in Canada. Most students attend public school.

Students over the age of 18 can live independently in their own accommodations (apartment or school residence). Living on campus in a residence after high school, for college or university studies is called *'living in residence'.*

WEATHER-THE MOST IMPORTANT INFORMATION TO KNOW WHILE IN CANADA

In Canada the weather changes quickly. Even in one day there can be four seasons. In the morning it can be sunny, in the afternoon it can rain and at night it can be snowy. The temperature can go up and down by 20 degrees in one day in any season.

Outdoor activities always depend on the weather. When it is sunny and warm, many people will hurry to go outside to enjoy the sun, especially in winter. But in winter, a sunny day with a blue sky can mean a very, very cold day. It can rain, snow, **hail** and be sunny in one day. Hail is small balls of ice that fall from the sky (sometimes even in summer) and freezing rain is cold hard rain that makes noise when it hits the window, the car or the road. It also stings when it hits your face. If you have never 'heard' weather, you will in Canada.

TIME CHANGES

There is a time change twice a year. In the spring the clock is put ahead one hour for Daylight Savings Time. In the fall, the clock is set back one hour to Standard Time. There is less daylight in winter (sometime only 6 hours) and more daylight in summer (up to 16 hours). The day this time change occurs varies every year.

Computers and cell phones adjust automatically if the Daylight Savings feature is turned on and the time zone is set to your location. Otherwise, radio, television, internet and newspapers will give reminders to people to set the time forward or backward.

SEASONS

Winter is from December 21 until March 20, spring is from March 21 to June 20, summer is from June 21 to September 20 and fall is September 21 to December 20.

Because there is less sunlight in the fall and winter time, many people take vitamin D pills. Some people use special lamps to help keep the good effects of light every day for more energy. When it is dark for most of the day with no sun for many days and it is cold, it makes people tired, sleepy and hungry.

As it gets closer to December 21, the days get shorter and it can become dark at 4 pm in the afternoon. Sometimes the sun will rise only at 7:45 am, which makes it necessary to have an alarm to wake people up in the morning for work and school. In Canada, time is marked by a twelve-hour system: (am) during the night and morning times, and (pm) for the afternoon and evening. For example, we say '8 am' for the morning and '8 pm' for the evening.

Temperature – Since the weather can change very much during the day it is important to check the weather forecast in the morning. Take an umbrella in case of rain, a jacket for wind, a sweater or coat, and in winter you must wear boots, have a hat and mitts and a winter coat all the time. Sometimes after a long period of cold weather, it will warm up but then it will get cold again. Weather is very unpredictable and being prepared with the correct clothing every day is very important.

To check the weather, it is good to have a weather application (app) on your cellphone. Check it when you wake up in the morning to decide what to wear and what to take with you. It is easy to get sick if you are not prepared for the type of weather. Catching a cold or the flu is common in fall and winter.

You must also know that the temperature is listed in two ways: the actual temperature and the 'windchill factor'. The windchill factor is the temperature, plus the wind, which makes it colder. Always dress to the windchill factor or the temperature shown 'with the wind' or 'feels like'.

In the summer the temperature is listed as the actual temperature and with 'the humidex' which means it will feel warmer because of the humidity (moisture) in the air. In the winter the humidity makes it feel colder than the actual temperature.

You will often be late to school because of weather. When it rains or snows or there is other bad weather, it affects the transportation. Cars and buses slow down because the roads get icy and slippery. You must be careful crossing the street because it takes longer for cars to stop on slippery roads. Always obey the pedestrian signals for crossing the street at a street corner. Look at the drivers to make sure they see you, if there is no light to help you cross safely.

'Snow days' mean no yellow school buses are running but schools are open. Some students stay home as teachers will not teach new material in class that day if the buses are late or not running, since many students cannot get to school (elementary and high school).

SAFETY TIP: Listening to music on headphones or texting is not safe when crossing the street because you need to hear traffic and look at drivers to make sure they see you.

Canadians are always talking about the weather because it decides what activity they will do that day.

CLOTHING

It is important to wear the right clothes for the right weather in Canada.

In the summer, many people wear cotton T-shirts and shorts, dresses or skirts but you will need a sweater or a sweatshirt at night if it gets cool.

Sometimes in air-conditioned shopping malls or homes it is very cool and you will need a light sweater.

Layering - An important concept to know is 'layering' your clothing which means to always have extra clothing that you can put on if you feel cold, or to take off if you feel warm.

Canadians will add a layer of clothing for every 10 degrees difference in temperature:

Summer- July/ August (20- 30°C): **1 layer** T-shirt, shorts, sweater at night (10 -15 degrees)

Fall -September/October (10-20°C): T-shirt, shorts with a sweater and sweatshirt or long pants, jeans and socks in shoes **(2 layers)**

Late fall -November to early December (0-10°C) T-shirt, sweater or sweatshirt and jacket or windbreaker, thin hat and thin mittens or gloves **(3 layers)**

Winter – mid December to end of February (-20 to 0 °C) T-shirt or thermal underwear, long sleeve shirt, sweatshirt and winter coat. Long underwear and pants, thick socks and winter boots **(4 layers)**

Spring- March-May – same as late fall and fall

At night in the winter, many people wear long sleeve pyjamas and long pant pyjamas.

SNOW AND ICE AND PROPER FOOTWEAR

Shoes are worn in spring, summer and fall. Boots are worn in late fall when the wind and rain are cold and shoes are not enough to keep your feet warm and dry. Boots are worn in winter to keep feet warm and dry from snow, **slush** and salt from the sidewalk and roads, which is used to melt the ice. Some people put 'ice cleats' on the bottom of their boots to walk safely on ice.

Wearing shoes when it is cold or snowy or icy can cause you to slip and fall and get hurt. Most people keep shoes for inside school, gym, office or home when there is snow on the ground.

Some families may ask you to help shovel snow when winter comes and wearing less layers under a coat is enough, because snow shoveling is hard work and you can get warm.

CLOTHING TIPS

- Buy boots, hats and gloves or mittens before winter as they **sell out** in stores

- Buy **fleece** or **wool blended** winter clothing because cotton clothing will not keep you warm in winter

- Heavy cotton sweatshirts or pants that are lined with fleece are comfortable and warm in winter

- Always take your coat off inside a building (school, home or shopping mall) as coats are considered outside clothing. Wear a sweater or sweatshirt if you feel cold inside. If you keep all your layers of clothing on inside, you will feel cold when you go back outside and have to wait for a bus.

- Have enough clothing to last 7 days or one week in every season, as most families only allow washing clothes once a week

CUSTOMS AND CULTURAL TRANSITIONING

If you wear a coat inside in a family's home it may be considered impolite, as it implies that the person's home is too cold for you.

Wearing a coat inside may also be considered impolite by some families because it may be interpreted that you will not be staying long and it may signal to the person that you do not feel welcome in his or her home.

Wear a **sweater or sweatshirt** if you feel cold inside a home or at school. It will show that you know how to adapt to how Canadians wear clothes in different seasons.

Always look to see how others are dressed and ask what to wear if you are unsure of the weather. You will feel more comfortable having more clothing than you need, instead of feeling cold if you do not have the correct clothing for that day.

Taking your shoes off at the door and lining up shoes neatly is also considered polite manners. Some families wear slippers in their home in the winter to keep feet warm but many homes have carpeting. In those homes, family members walk around with only socks on their feet.

GOOD TABLE MANNERS:

- Come right away when you are called to eat with the family

- Take a baseball cap off your head at the table when eating

- Ask where you may sit at the table when it is your first time eating at someone's house. In many families, certain members of the family always sit in the same place at the table.

- Use a spoon or fork to serve onto your plate from the serving dish; do not put your fork or spoon in the serving dish and then to your mouth; some families 'plate the food' from the stove if there is a small kitchen table. Other families put the food on the table in serving dishes so that every one can help themselves to choose what they wish to eat on their own plate

- Say 'excuse me' if you happen to burp or flatulate at the dinner table or anywhere in public. Burping, flatulating and/or spitting in public is not good manners.

- Say *'excuse me'* when reaching over someone at the table to get an item or say *'please pass me the dish'*

- Don't put your head down and your mouth on the plate or slurp food from the plate into your mouth

- Use a spoon or fork to lift food to your mouth or lift the bowl up to your mouth to drink from it

- Chew with your mouth closed and wipe your mouth with a paper napkin

- When you are finished eating line up the fork and knife on the side of the plate and say *'thank you for the breakfast/lunch or supper/dinner'* when you have finished eating

- To ask to leave the table say *'may I be excused?'*

- Some families eat with their hands and have different table habits and manners; always watch what the adults do, or ask, if you are not sure of how to do something at the table

- Push your chair in under the table as you leave the table

- Put your used dishes where your host indicates (on the kitchen counter, in the kitchen sink or in the dishwasher)

- Keep your cellphone in your pocket at the table if there is another person at the table at the same time as you; it is acceptable to take it out and use it if you are eating alone

- Wipe off the table with a sink cloth after eating or brush the crumbs into your hand and put them in the garbage to leave the table surface clean after yourself

- Use the same drinking glass for water during the day and not a new one each time, except for juice, milk or another type of drink when you can take a clean glass

- Engage in table conversation when others are at the table. If you do not speak, your host will think you are angry, sad, sick or there is a problem or you are not friendly. Tell about your day and ask questions about what you find different in your new life and talk about your home and your family

- If you are eating alone in the kitchen and want to heat up food in the microwave, use the plastic microwave '**splatter cover**' (plastic cover) over your plate of food, so that food pieces do not dirty the inside of the microwave as your food is heating.

Eating with other students at school is sometimes different than eating with adults at a family table setting. By watching what others do and say, you can learn the customs quickly.

> **Note: it is not common in Canadian families to have paid cooks or housekeepers or maids as part of the household. Mothers or fathers**

> in each family will cook or clean the house. You should not expect that someone will make food for you three times a day. You will be expected to make food for yourself if you are hungry.

MEALTIMES

Breakfast - During the week from Monday to Friday, breakfast can be from 5:30 am to 9 am as families get ready for work and school. You will be expected to get your own breakfast and prepare your own lunch for school at breakfast time, or the night before, after supper. Most Canadians eat a quick breakfast such as toast or cereal, a bagel or muffin. Families do not often sit down together to eat at this time.

On Saturdays and Sundays, people enjoy big breakfasts and take their time to eat more and enjoy sitting together to share this meal with friends or family. These meals can include more food with bacon, sausages, eggs, toast, pancakes, waffles, cheese and fruit. Breakfast between 10 am and 2 pm is called **brunch** and some restaurants have a set menu or buffet only during these times. You may be introduced to Maple Syrup, a Canadian natural tree product, which is often served with weekend breakfast food.

Lunch –Lunch is usually a quick meal during weekdays and on weekends, unless a family goes to a restaurant. Lunch hours are usually between 11 am and 1 pm.

On school days, students take their own lunch using a lunch bag. They may make a sandwich in the morning, take fruit, cookies and a water bottle or juice box, or take leftovers to heat up in a microwave at school. High schools, colleges and universities have cafeterias with food available, but it is not often high quality and can be expensive.

It is a Canadian custom to eat **leftovers** the next day, usually from food that is left uneaten from supper the day before. This food is packed in a plastic dish and reheated in a microwave oven and is called a **hot lunch**.

Dinner or Supper- Dinner or supper is usually between 5 pm and 7 pm and this is usually the one meal each day that families will sit down and eat together; but in some busy families, this custom may only happen on weekends. Some Canadian families have **fast food** for supper on weekdays, which is bought on the way home from work or school. Other families make supper from frozen food which is baked, boiled or fried. Few families cook a meal from fresh ingredients during the week because it takes too long to prepare, unless one adult is at home to make it. A few families only cook meals on weekends and reheat this food for meals during the week.

You may be asked to help out with some household tasks, which are called '**chores**'. Families living in a house will have appliances to help with the chores, such as a dishwasher in the kitchen and a washing machine and a dryer for laundering clothes, upstairs, on the main floor or in the basement. Some families hire a cleaning service once or twice a month to clean the house but this is considered a luxury.

FOOD IN CANADA

Ready to eat food from a garden or field is limited in Canada, and if it is grown, it will be in the summer months of July and August. Locally grown food can be vegetables (potatoes, carrots, beets, cabbage, lettuce, broccoli and cauliflower) or fruits (apples, pears, peaches, strawberries, blueberries, raspberries, blackberries). Since much food has to be brought to Canada especially in the winter, it is very expensive to buy fresh fruit and vegetables.

Families will eat a lot of bread and pasta (noodles in different shapes and size) and pizza is a quick food and a favourite of young people.

Meat is cooked outdoors on natural gas or propane fuelled barbeque grills in the summer and is usually steak, hot dogs and hamburgers. Meat is eaten several times a week but not always every day in every family. Most meat eaten is chicken, pork and beef.

Many families buy frozen food and use it throughout the week as some families only buy food once a week. This trip to the food store is called 'doing the groceries'.

Canadian food and family eating customs are usually plain, fast and simple and the object is to be able to make a quick meal to eat. Some families focus on healthy eating and will cook a fresh meal every day. Every family is different but it will likely be a very different experience than what you are used to at home in your country. You may also enjoy some excellent meals at good restaurants with your friends while you are in Canada.

CANADIAN HOMES

DOING LAUNDRY

Families usually wash their clothes once a week in a washing machine, either top loaded or side loaded.

Clothes are separated into different piles: whites, colours, darks and sometimes by weight and colour and placed one by one into the machine. Hot, warm or cold water can be chosen for the water temperature. It usually takes 40 to 60 minutes for a load of laundry to be washed.

Clothes are usually dried in a dryer. It usually takes 40 to 60 minutes for a load of laundry to be dry in the dryer. If clothes are hung up to dry, it will be beside the washing machine in the laundry room or another area of the house. In general, families will not allow clothes to be hung up for drying in the bedroom.

> **Note: Ask how to use the washer and dryer and where you may hang clothes to dry if you do not wish to put them in the dryer. In some Canadian cities it is not permitted to dry clothes outside. Outside of cities, clothes can be dried outside.**

You may be asked to do your laundry on a particular day of the week at a set time because it is less expensive to do laundry after 7pm in the evening and on weekends. Canadians pay for electricity, heat and water in their homes and these costs can be high at certain times. Appliances are run in the evenings to keep costs down.

Your bed may have a top and bottom sheet or a bottom sheet and a duvet cover. Your bedding (sheets and pillow cases) should be washed or changed regularly. Ask your host family when this should be done (usually every two weeks).

IN THE BATHROOM

You will be expected to take a shower every day, either in the morning or in the evening. Sometimes in the summer, family members shower twice a day if it is very hot outside.

Smelling fresh and clean is very important and wearing deodorant is expected, in consideration of the people around you and family members in your home.

You are expected to provide your own **toiletries** (shampoo, soap, toothpaste).

> Note: It is important to know that the custom is to leave the bathroom door open when no one is using the bathroom. If the door is closed, it means someone is inside.

In some homes, leaving the bathroom door open is important for proper air circulation and ventilation, as not all bathrooms have windows in many homes. Bathrooms which have no windows have a fan inside the ceiling to take moisture out.

GOOD MANNERS WHEN SHARING A BATHROOM WITH OTHER PEOPLE:

- Always turn the **ceiling fan on** when taking a shower. The fan switch is beside the light switch by the door. Leave the fan on until you are finished in the bathroom.

- Take a short shower (no longer than 10 minutes) if there are many people in the home.

- It is proper to wipe off the bathroom counter and not leave water for the next person.

- When taking a shower be mindful to put the curtain lining INSIDE the tub so as to keep the water inside the tub and not on the bathroom floor.

- Also make sure there is no water on the floor by wiping it up with the floor towel in front of the bathtub. Water on the floor may cause someone to slip and fall.

Toilets may be single flush or double flush to save water. A double flush toilet has a button or **lever** to flush a small amount of water one way (to flush urine) and more water the other way (for stool or feces). Girls and women must use the double flush if flushing a tampon in the toilet.

> Note: Only toilet paper and tampons can be flushed in a toilet. Paper tissues, condoms

> and feminine sanitary napkins must go in the garbage bin in the bathroom. Please wrap these items in toilet paper before putting them in the garbage to be discreet with personally used items.

Men and boys put up the toilet seat when they urinate. Always flush the toilet after use.

Your host may ask you not to flush the toilet if you go to the bathroom during the night, so that the noise does not wake up other members of the household who are sleeping. Flush it in the morning. Some host families may ask that you keep the toilet seat lid down for sanitary reasons. It is best to leave the bathroom the way you found it when you went in.

IN THE BEDROOM

When you are in your bedroom and someone knocks at the door, it is polite to get up and open the door for the person. You can also call out *'Yes?'* or *'Come in'* in a loud voice which gives permission for the person to open the door and speak to you directly. Speaking to someone through a closed door is considered impolite.

Some families may not allow food in the bedroom. Since many homes in Canada are made out of wood under brick, there are often bugs which enter the house in all seasons. Having food in the bedroom may invite bugs into your space. If your room has carpeting the host may not allow food because of spills and stains that are difficult to clean on carpet.

Your host family will likely communicate specific rules about food in the bedroom.

Keeping your room reasonably tidy is respecting the environment.

Electricity voltage is 110V for plugging in electronics.

> **Note: It is best to purchase an adapter and laptops and phones in Canada. Do not bring a converter made in China (below) as these are not safe for Canadian homes, even though it may indicate the correct voltage. Improper use of converters and electronics may cause fires. Fire is always a big danger to Canadians and their homes.**

You may be allowed to put up decorations in your room if your host family allows it, but you must check with your host family before doing so. Bringing pictures of your family, a favourite souvenir, a sentimental object or any other items which would make you feel more comfortable is welcome in your space.

Canadian children and teenagers also love having **sleepovers**. This custom means you can invite a friend to sleep in your bedroom for one night or you may be invited to sleep at a friend's house for one night. If you are invited over you can bring a **sleeping bag** and a pillow with you. If a friend sleeps over they usually sleep on the floor, on an inflatable mattress or camping cot in your room. Sometimes sleepovers are held in the **family room** where there may be an extra **sofa bed**. Homestay rules in general do not allow boys to sleep at girls' homes or girls to sleep at boys' homes.

EXPRESSIONS RELATED TO HOMES

Sleeping bag – a zippered blanket bag usually used for camping outdoors but indoors as bedding

Family room – a room on the main floor or in the basement of a home where families gather to watch television or movies and play video games. If many kids sleep over they will usually stay in this room to watch a movie, eat popcorn and talk until everyone falls asleep here, mainly on the floor.

Sofa bed – a couch that opens up into a bed usually for two people. A sofa bed is most commonly used as a temporary bed for guests sleeping over at a home. It can also be found in the main living area upstairs or in the family room downstairs in the basement.

In Canada it is common to use the basement of a home as a living space, usually for entertainment. Some homes have bedrooms in the basement usually for older adult children or teenagers who want their own space away from the rest of the family. Some basements are also used as apartments with a kitchen and a bathroom.

Basements used as living spaces are referred to as 'finished basements'. If a home's basement is not finished as a living space it is called an 'unfinished basement' and is usually used for storage.

Windows and some doors in homes usually have screens to keep out the insects which crawl or fly into the house in the summer time. Canada is a country with lots of bugs or insects, so screens help to keep these bugs outdoors. It is polite to always close doors or if they are left open, and to close the screen door.

Fresh air is important and many families like to have their doors and windows open, sometimes even in winter for a short period of time to air out the house. The air is often clean (especially outside of large cities) and helps to freshen the home and exchange the air in the house.

If the home has **central air conditioning**, you will be asked to keep the windows closed at all times.

> NOTE: Turn off the lights when you are not in a room as electricity costs are high for families.

Recycling garbage – Each city in Canada has its own rules for recycling but it is very important that you dispose of your garbage in the correct way during your stay in Canada. Many communities in Canada separate plastic, glass, paper and trash. Your host will ask you to recycle your garbage and show you how to use the **blue bin, black bin, green bin and garbage cans for trash**.

Cities and citizens are proud to protect the environment in Canada and it is a cultural value. It is expected that you will follow the recycling habits of the family where you stay.

> **FIRE SAFETY** -Since most homes in Canada are made of wood and brick there is a smoke alarm in every home. Look for this alarm when you arrive and have your host show you how it sounds. If you hear the alarm ALWAYS LEAVE YOUR ROOM and go outside, <u>even in winter,</u> unless your host indicates that the alarm went off from cooking smoke. If a real fire existed you have 3 minutes to get out of a house in Canada to save your life.

 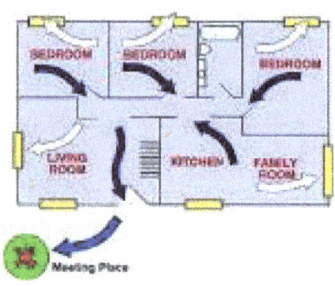

> Fire is the most dangerous event in a Canadian home. You should ask your host to show you the fire escape plan from your room. There should always be two ways for you to escape from a home.

EMERGENCY- If you ever see smoke or fire **call 911** and give your address. This number is used to reach police, firefighters and ambulance.

Temperature in a home – most Canadian homes are air conditioned in the summer to 20 or 23 degrees and heated in the winter to about the same temperature. Many families lower the **thermostat** in the home at night to 16 or 18 degrees and use more blankets and **duvets** to keep warm. If you are cold in the home make sure your window is tightly closed and wear a sweater or sweatshirt (2 layers). Sometimes a home may feel cold even if it is 20 degrees because of the humidity.

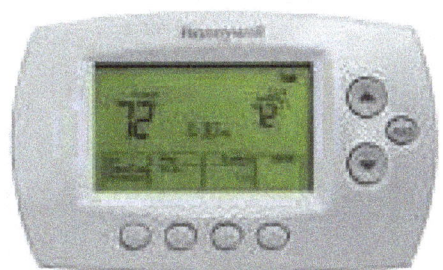

Some homes have gas or wood burning fireplaces for extra warmth or decoration in winter.

COMMUNICATION AND SPOKEN EXPRESSIONS

Communicating is an important skill in Canada and you will be expected to tell your host everything, good or bad. If you like something in your home or that your host does, please say so. It helps the host understand your likes and dislikes.

If you do not like something in your home or that your host does, it is also important that you tell your host. It is not considered rude or impolite to indicate if something bothers you or makes you uncomfortable.

Say *'excuse me but I need to tell you that something bothers me'* and then explain what it is.

When you first arrive, it is important to use YES and NO to answer questions from your host and to communicate with everyone. Avoid using expressions like **'ya' 'ok' 'sure' 'maybe'** as these can be confusing in communication at the beginning because they all mean YES but are used in different ways.

Canadians are very polite people so

- ✓ use **please** when you ask for anything
- ✓ and **thank you** every time you receive information, objects or advice.

Most families will ask you to call the adults by their first name and not use titles such as Mr. Mrs, Miss or Ms. which is usually used only in writing. It is very formal to use these in spoken language and it may make some people uncomfortable.

If you are not sure how to call an adult, ask

'How may I address you?'

Canadians also apologize a lot in their social interactions. Say '**sorry**' if you

- make a mistake
- forget something
- bump into someone
- misunderstand a message
- don't understand what is expected of you

Ask the person to repeat what he or she has said by saying

'I'm sorry, can you repeat that please?' or *'Pardon?'*

Note: Saying 'what?' is considered rude.

Also look at the person talking to you, not down at your phone or away from the person.

When you enter or leave a house and there is someone still at home, call out to say you are leaving,

'bye, I'm going now, see you later' or

when arriving back say

'hello! I'm back, or *'I'm home'*.

Often people will ask how you are in the morning,

'Good morning, how are you? How did you sleep?'

or at the end of the day they will ask how your day was

'How was your day?'

It is polite to answer in more than one sentence and not just say, *'fine'*.

Say, *'my day was good or interesting'* and tell something about your day.

Your host will be interested to know how your day went and what was interesting, funny, challenging or new to you. Having a brief exchange with another person when you come in, is important to show that you are interested in being a member of the family.

> **Note: Do not get offended if someone corrects the way you say something in English. It is meant to help you integrate into the language and culture more easily, or to communicate your message more clearly.**

If you come into the home and you are listening to music, take out your **earbuds** from your ears, or take off your **headphones,** just like you take off your coat, shoes, boots, hat and mittens and then greet the person or people in the home.

Also, if something breaks in your room let your host know right away. If your host discovers it when you have left it could make them angry because it will cost more to fix over time.

CELLPHONE USE AND TEXTING

When you are in Canada, you will need to obtain a cellphone plan with a Canadian phone number. You can buy different plans but if you choose one with data, you must know that Canada a limited 4G network. Your home may have an internet plan but it may not be unlimited so ask your host about internet use when you arrive.

Most hosts expect you to call or text a message to them for communication, but not when you are at home in the house. If is not considered polite to text a person in the same house when he or she is present. Go speak to him or her face to face.

When you receive a text from your host, always respond so that your host knows you have read the message. This exchange is called 'texting etiquette', which means polite use of your cellphone, as if it was a conversation.

If you do not respond to a message it would be like you are ignoring the person which is considered rude. You do not need to respond immediately, just as long as you respond when you read the message.

NON-VERBAL COMMUNICATION

Facial expressions, gestures and body language- many Canadians will communicate their feelings or mood by nonverbal behaviour through their facial expression, gesture (moving their hands around) or body language (how they move their body either standing, walking or sitting).

If someone is sitting, quiet, does not look at you and does not respond, it usually means he or she is busy or wants to be alone, so do not bother him or her.

Hugging and kissing- many teenagers, especially girls, will openly hug friends as part of their greeting to each other. Boys may hug, **'high five'** or **'fist pump'** or tap shoulders. Some people may give a kiss on one cheek or both cheeks. People who are romantically attracted may kiss on the lips in public and hold hands.

It is not acceptable to physically push or hit a person in public as this may be considered assault.

People who are rude, bullying, teasing or make you uncomfortable need to be reported to an adult. Do not accept or tolerate any unwelcome behaviour from another person at any time. If you are on the bus, tell the bus driver if someone is bothering you.

ASKING QUESTIONS FOR MORE INFORMATION IS VERY IMPORTANT IN CANADA

Expressions related to asking:

'if you don't ask, you don't get' – means if you don't initiate a question you may not receive something that would be of benefit to you, for example, a store discount in the price of an item, an extra piece of meat at the dinner table, an extra chance to raise your mark in a school subject. It is the same as a lost opportunity to gain something favorable.

'if you snooze, you lose' – means if you take too long to decide, you may lose an opportunity to also gain something favourable to you.

'always ask, the worst they can say is no' – means that there is no shame or harm in asking, even if you think you may not obtain something; sometimes, by asking, you can be pleasantly surprised by the response you receive.

TRANSPORTATION AND TRAVEL

In Canada most families will have one or two cars as it is the most common way to get from home to school or work. Students will either walk, take a yellow school bus or public transportation to school. Some parents will drive their children to school. In the spring and fall some students may ride their bicycle to get to school. These bikes are locked using a combination lock outside of the front of the school during the day.

If you are traveling between cities, you may go by intercity bus or train or to larger cities further away, by plane. Most students take the bus as it is the least expensive way to travel. The train is not always reliable in its schedule and most people drive or fly for greater distances.

Most Canadians live within 200 km of the border with the United States. You may need a US visa if you wish to cross the border from Canada to the USA with friends or family.

> **Note:** You must always wear a seat belt when travelling in a car. It is the law and you can be fined (have to pay money) as a passenger, or if you are under 18 years of age, the adult driver is fined. All passengers and drivers must wear seatbelts in Canada in the front and rear seats of a vehicle.

SCHOOLS IN CANADA

High schools can be for students aged 12- 18 and range from grade 7 to 12. Some high schools only have students from grades 9-12 (ages 14-18). All high schools have classrooms, a science laboratory, computer laboratory, library, gymnasium and cafeteria. Some schools may have one floor or two floors.

Libraries in schools are now called **learning commons** and different areas are for quiet study or group work. No food or drink is generally allowed in a library or computer lab. There may be couches or comfortable seats for reading and studying.

In classrooms, there can be desks and chairs, tables and chairs or seats with a small writing surface attached and a basket underneath to place items. Most classrooms have a **Smartboard** but some may still have black or green boards used with chalk, or white boards used with markers.

Every student is assigned a locker, and you must buy a **combination lock** to use it. Inside there are hooks for your coat and a shelf for books or other items. Many students purchase plastic organizers to place inside to keep things neat and tidy. Students often decorate the inside of the locker door with favourite pictures or a mirror or other special items. Sometimes the outside of a locker may be decorated by friends if it is that student's birthday.

Colleges and universities also have lockers for students but fewer students use these as most adult students bring their belongings around with them in a **knapsack** or **backpack**.

Indoor shoes – some schools require students to have a pair of indoor shoes during the winter and do not allow students to walk around in boots inside the school. It is also not appropriate to wear your coat inside a classroom and a teacher may ask you to return it to your locker. Wear a sweater or sweatshirt inside the school if you feel cold. All schools are heated in winter in Canada but are not always warm.

Non-marking soled sports shoes are mandatory in all gymnasiums for sports, whether school, college, university or public or private gymnasiums (gyms).

It is expected that students ask questions in class from the teacher and it is a standard to which good students are held. A good student is a student who asks lots of questions because it means that the student is interested in learning and is participating in his or her learning. Teachers like students who ask questions.

Explicit versus implicit instruction – sometimes a teacher will expect that you know something that may have been taught in previous years and will not know if you are having difficulty. Observing to learn from others, is an important skill to use in school.

Some teachers expect you to work with other students to learn from each other and group work or assignments or projects are given so that every person in the group can help with the final outcome. Giving presentations in front of the class is also very common and usually a part of a group or individual project.

Tests, assessments and examinations (exams) are always individual and you are not allowed to communicate with a classmate during such tasks. Sharing notes or information during a test is associated with cheating and your mark may be affected or you may be asked to leave the class and not be able to complete the test. There are always consequences to cheating at schools and you may be asked to go see the school principal.

School rules and the teachers' instructions must always be followed. Consequences may vary from teacher to teacher and school to school, but may include suspension from school or an extra task.

College and universities may **expel** a student for cheating with no reimbursement for tuition paid.

Plagiarism is also considered a serious **academic offense**. You cannot 'copy and paste' information you find on the internet into your school work unless you also copy the link you used to find the information.

Always ask to know the rules as soon as you start school. These rules are called the **Student Code of Conduct**. They may also include what type of clothes you are allowed and not allowed to wear at school.

Many students engage in extracurricular activities at school which may include clubs. Sports teams and fun activities are also available to participate in at a high school, college and university. Tryouts are done for teams which represent the school but playing a sport for fun is called a **house league** and anyone can join. These activities are usually held at lunch time or after school. Sports teams will often practice in the early morning before classes start or after the school day ends.

Some young people have extracurricular activities that are not school related. These can be sports teams, music classes, cultural activities or volunteering. All high school students must complete volunteer hours in the community as part of the high school diploma, but each province or territory decides how many hours are required (generally between 25 and 40 hours).

ATTITUDE AND MOTIVATION FOR A SUCCESSFUL EXPERIENCE

It is important to come to Canada to study with an open mind, which means you are ready to face different ways of learning and living every day. It may be very difficult at the beginning but asking questions and asking for help are very important for being successful.

Students who progress well in school adapt quickly to the way students in Canada dress, eat, play, speak and learn. Trying different foods is a good way to show your interest to your host.

It is appropriate to say you do not like something, but only after you have tried it.

Some students encounter more relaxed rules when they come to Canada and forget good habits they learned in schools in the home country. Hosts and schools in Canada will expect students to be responsible and independent which means knowing what to do without reminding. Also, once you are asked to do something a particular way, to continue doing it, without being told again. It usually takes three weeks to learn a new habit and most Canadian families will be patient to teach you new ways of doing things.

If a student comes to study but does not have good study habits it will be difficult and not a successful experience. Students who have trouble in school at home will have trouble in school in Canada. Problems do not disappear because you are studying in a new country.

Some students come to Canada unwillingly, perhaps because their parents wanted them to come to learn the language. This situation is not good and will result in poor success and much frustration.

Successful students are flexible, adventurous, adaptable, reasonable, courteous and respectful and want to learn and study in English. If the level of English language skills is not sufficient, it is a setback to studies. All school work must be submitted in English at Canadian schools (or in French if it is a French language school where the student attends) including colleges and universities.

STAYING HEALTHY WHILE IN CANADA

It is very important that students stay healthy while they live and study in Canada, especially in winter. Eating fruits and vegetables becomes harder as these may not taste the same as in the home country. Taking vitamin C and vitamin D tablets help maintain good health during the winter and it is common for Canadians to take supplements during the fall and winter seasons.

If you fall sick in Canada you may go to a walk-in clinic to see a doctor but you will have to pay upfront for the visit which may cost over $200. It is required to have your own medical insurance while you study in Canada. The insurance provider reimburses your cost to visit the doctor and medication you may need.

Hospitals are only used if there is an accident or a life- threatening condition (difficulty breathing, bleeding or broken bones). Doctors are the same quality and standard regardless if you see them in a clinic or hospital. All doctors are qualified and must follow the same rules of practice regardless of where they see patients. Hospitals can cost up to $800 for one visit for international students, so it is only in an emergency that you should go there.

Many medical clinics have 'after hours' or 'urgent care' services as well. Seeing a doctor during the night is possible without going to a hospital.

It is very important that you disclose to those that live with you if you have any medical conditions. It is your responsibility to tell your host or living companions if you have a health problem. In case of a medical emergency, the doctors, nurses and paramedics need to know allergies, medications and serious health problems (heart conditions, asthma, diabetes etc) that you may have, in order to treat you correctly based on your symptoms.

In winter it is especially important to eat and sleep enough and to dress warm. Some students get **flu shots**, which are vaccines to prevent influenza. Dry skin is also a common problem so people use skin cream and body lotion after a shower and lip balm to soothe dry lips from the cold.

PERSONAL SAFETY

While in Canada you will be expected to follow all federal (national), provincial or territorial and municipal (city) laws. Local laws are important for you to know and it is your responsibility to ask and learn them. These laws may be different in each region or city so ask your host or other students when you arrive. Some laws apply to people between the ages of 14 and 18.

Curfew is an important rule to follow if you are under 18 years of age. The curfew is the time that you must be home at night if you go out. It may be your host family's rule, a Homestay organization's rule or a local law. Find out what it is and respect it by being home on time.

When you first arrive, it is important that you come home before dark until you know your neighbourhood and the transportation system well. Many newcomers get lost when it is dark because surroundings look different.

Never carry more than $50-100 dollars with you at any time. Canadians do not carry cash with them and if you are stopped by the police or school officials and you have a large amount of cash with you, it may cause you difficulties. Many people who carry large amounts of cash are associated with drug trafficking or prostitution.

Once you receive your school timetable, go to a bank and open a Canadian bank account right away. You need a Canadian bank account to accept money transfers, use a debit or credit card and to keep your cash money safe. A student bank account does not cost money to open, keep or close and it is important for personal safety. International credit cards may not always work in all stores in Canada.

Canadian cities are generally safe to travel by public transportation. It is always a good idea to be home by 10 pm and travel with another friend if one lives near you, if you are out late at night.

Always tell your host if you are coming home late, or if you have a problem, so that you may get help or a ride if needed. Taxis and Ubers are available in larger cities in Canada.

You must always lock the front door of your home or apartment when you come in and when you leave. It is the safest way to protect you and your belongings and the family or people with whom you are staying.

These items are important to carry with you every day:

- Bus pass or
- Cash for bus, taxi or Uber (and purchasing food)
- Student identification card with photo (ID card) from the school you are attending

- Health insurance card
- Debit or credit card
- Your address and host's name in your cell phone contact list

Do not carry your passport with you every day. Keep it locked or in a safe place in your room.

SMOKING, ALCOHOL AND DRUGS

The legal age for smoking tobacco and drinking alcohol is different in each province of Canada. Check websites for the province and city where you will live to know the law. Marijuana (cannabis) for medicinal purposes is legal in Canada and recreational use is legal since October 2018. Separate laws apply to youth under the age of 18 for cannabis and you must know these laws. All other drugs are illegal in Canada. You must have your personal medication in prescribed containers when you bring these with you from your home country.

Enjoy your stay and study experience in Canada. Take time to visit places and learn from experiences outside of school. Most of all, make new friends and contacts as they may lead to other new experiences and maybe even a future job or career in Canada.

ABOUT THE AUTHOR

Monika Ferenczy is an Education Consultant who helps students and parents make decisions regarding learning and education. Her practice focuses on finding the best solution to meet the needs of students, young or mature, to help them reach their full potential. Providing relevant and timely information is critical for sound decision-making and she assists all Canadian and international clients with the highest quality of service. Considered an expert in the education sector, Monika supports families with special needs children, offers education expertise in separation and divorce proceedings, presents workshops for young parents and advocates for improved educational practices, policies and legislation to government.

CPSIA information can be obtained
at www.ICGtesting.com
Printed in the USA
BVHW011137300423
663291BV00013B/73/J